I am not from here

María do Cebreiro

I am not from here

translated by Helena Miguélez-Carballeira

Shearsman Books
Exeter

First published in the United Kingdom in 2010 by
Shearsman Books Ltd
58 Velwell Road
Exeter EX4 4LD

www.shearsman.com

ISBN 978-1-84861-111-5
First edition

Translation of *Non son de aquí*, published in Galician by
Edicións Xerais de Galicia, S.A., Vigo, 2008

Acknowledgements
The publication of this book has been funded by the Spanish
Ministerio de Ciencia e Innovación through the grant
FFI2009-08475/FILO for the study of contemporary Irish
and Galician women writers.

The translator would also like to thank her colleagues and friends
Zoë Skoulding and Kirsty Hooper for the kind help
they offered at the time she was preparing the manuscript.

We are grateful to Edicións Xerais de Galicia, S.A., Vigo,
for granting permission to issue this English translation.

Contents

'I am not from here':
A Translation for María do Cebreiro

Helena Miguélez Carballeira

> The ideal I'm envisioning here is a mind receptive
> to thoughts, able to nurture and connect them, and
> susceptible to happiness in their entertainment.
> Eve Kosfosky Sedgwick, *Touching Feeling.*

Theorists of nondualistic thought continue to puzzle over the persistence of binaries, even after almost four decades of direct critique of their limited scope for representation and disarming arbitrariness, and especially of the power differentials they rest upon. This perplexity has been fuelled in part by the particular pace and logic of post-structuralist study, sometimes dilatory, sometimes plain self-cancelling. Critics are now asking pointed questions which acknowledge the continuing need for work that identifies essentialism in its many guises and complicates our understanding of it. But these voices nevertheless show an impatience with the fact that alternative visions have not been forthcoming and that a 'truly' nondualistic critical practice, one that is alert even to the potentially bipolar narratives underlying inclusive and constructivist theoretical projects (those orbiting around performativities, genealogies and total histories, to name just a few of the most fertile), is simply quite hard to achieve. Luckily for those of us whose hearts are made lighter through strenuous dialogue with the unintelligible, there are now some phenomenally articulate voices envisaging (and tentatively communicating) new directions.[1] The proposed pathways seem to be turning more and more into nerve-ways, drifting away from the insights that joined world structures to bodies, and into new perceptive stances that join bodies to bodies, minds to minds: a poetics of propinquity and affect, a preoccupation not so much with *beneath*, but as Eve Kosofsky Sedgwick has put it, with *beside* (2003: 8). We are not oblivious to the fact that

7

this revelation of a powerful correlation between cognition and affect comes at a taxing time for human sensitivity. We are constantly exposed to narratives of loss: loss of the language we speak, of stretches of undefiled coastline, of the possibility of self and of selflessness. In their sheer ubiquity, these narratives inure us against the risk of pain and prepare us for the world without us, which Alan Weisman has so forcibly drawn (2007). And yet, perhaps, the sense of urgency we derive from being fully enmeshed with processes of irreversible damage is the reason why rational activity has become so people-oriented. Our fight against destitution, too, seems a struggle for collective self-forgiveness: a difficult desideratum, and one perhaps made possible only in the blissful space afforded by reading, thinking and writing.

For some time now I have suspected that the work of poet and literary theorist María do Cebreiro (Santiago de Compostela, 1976) has grappled with these questions in ways that are at the very least triangular and which, importantly, do not evade the suggestion of answers. Since publishing her first book of poetry in 1998, *O estadio do espello* [The Mirror Stage], María do Cebreiro has revealed a creative capacity virtually unbound by the labeling and categorizing enterprise that so often characterizes work in the humanities. She is a dedicated poet and an influential literary theorist, currently based at the University of Santiago de Compostela (Galicia). Her scholarly output inhabits the interstices of critical theory, Hispanic and Galician studies with the kind of obstinacy that reveals a deeply felt commitment to interdisciplinary thought. Her critical and theoretical writing springs from an enormously sophisticated intimacy with ancient, modern and contemporary literatures, as well as intellectual history, delighting in a style spacious enough to house the esoteric and the plain to see. She has lit the way of theoretical paths previously uncharted in Galician studies (related to aspects of the spectral in Galician literature or to the role and status of *traducións de autor* in the Galician cultural field, to name two of her most recent projects), while remaining a key commentator in ongoing cultural debates, such as those revolving around the nation and nationalism, or the instrumentalised role of women-authored literature.

As a poet, her trajectory has gathered a particular form of (sustained) momentum, at a time when Galician female-authored poetry is being hailed as a long-due literary event. Critics have said of her contemporaries that they disassembled language through the venting of bottled-up drives, contained in a collective female body which had until that moment (the 1990s) remained almost anaemic with neglect. Poets such as Yolanda Castaño, Lupe Gómez or María Lado spoke of fickle instincts, breasts and anorexia. In so doing they told a different story to that traditionally allotted women in Galician historical discourse, with its ingrained sentimentalisation of their capacity for labour and endurance, their robustness and sturdy beauty. While these poets' projects were distinctively engaged and provocative, criticism, even when it aims to publicise their achievements, rarely considers their idiosyncratic features. Radically different poetic voices have been measured by the same gauge, perhaps with the intention to augment their literary force through a celebration of coherence. That their coherence as a 'group' (a 'generation' even, as some put it) may have been slightly contrived is a suspicion that has only recently begun to emerge.

In her capacity as both agent and observer, María do Cebreiro's poetic and academic work has provided key responses to the above processes. She has, for example, single-handedly questioned whether literary recourse to the body in Galician female-authored poetry in the nineties had been a veritably political gesture (Rábade Villar 2008). Her explanation of how it was not looked inward at her own creative practice but was also meant to interrogate a critical environment that sees any form of female-authored creative dialogue with notions such as privacy, sexuality and the body as engaged and political by default. The effects of such critical workings, she has warned, are just as indicative of a restrictive reading of women's literature (one still resting upon untheorised notions of respectability) as they are of an impoverished understanding of what it takes to be political and to write politically. In her bold definition of what such an undertaking entails, the poet and the critic's voice come together with the kind of conceptual sharpness that is more characteristic of careful reflection than of impulse.

But María do Cebreiro's poetry is not preoccupied with drives. I have drawn for this realization on the work of psychologist of emotions Silvain S. Tomkins and his ground-breaking, yet little known distinction between drives and affects.[2] Although it is not the place here to delve deeply into Tomkin's work, let us establish at least the following. Freudian and post-Freudian psychology have tended to subordinate affective responsive structures in human psychology to the governing urgency of primary drives, which, by way of this hierarchical logic, are endowed with greater explanatory power. An acute reader of Tomkins' work, Kosfosky Sedgwick has explained his challenge to this widespread view as follows:

> 'Common sense holds [...] that the drive system is the primary motivator of human behavior, to which the affects are inevitably secondary. Tomkins shows the opposite to be true: that motivation itself, even the motivation to satisfy biological drives, is the business of the affect system.'
> (2003: 20)

I see the above as a theoretical *tour de force* and one whose profound implications for the so-called 'affective turn' in political and sociocultural sciences has been seldom considered. I seize it for this analysis of contemporary female-authored poetry in Galicia, and especially María do Cebreiro's work, because Tomkins' distinction between drive and affect suggests to me the possibility of a dividing line between the main shared concerns of Galician women poets writing in the nineties and María do Cebreiro's work today. For if Yolanda Castaño's *yolandolatría* or Olga Novo's *líquidos íntimos* stemmed from a preoccupation with the poetic expression of contradictory, self-absorbed or unfettered passions, in an attempt to jostle Galician readers into recognising the possibility of an intransigent female body, María do Cebreiro's poetry places passions not against a cognitive tradition that has historically cast them aside as volatile or mundane, but as part and parcel of a new cognitive order conducive to new political possibilities. In her poetry, reason and emotion cease to relate to each other in a dualistic and hierarchical fashion, giving way instead to affective forms of understanding that not only drive, but also result from what Patricia Ticineto Clough has termed a 'felt vitality', a 'felt aliveness' (Clough 2007:2). It is in this sense that I would argue that María do Cebreiro's work, so far available almost exclusively in its original Galician language, enters fully into dialogue with the very contemporary insight that 'powerful emotions have an irreducibly important cognitive role to play' (Nussbaum 1990:7). My reference to Martha C. Nussbaum's work is also evocative of what I consider an equally central aspect of María do Cebreiro's inquiry as a 'thinker-poet' (15), namely that certain truths about human life can be approximated only through poetic language. An unabashed attachment to ethics is not difficult to detect in such a reading of her project. Ethics, however, is to be understood in her writing as a commitment to dialogue with the many manifestations of affect in human existence, with our capacity to affect and be affected, and to sustain this dialogue even in the face of the elusive nature of the notions upon which it rests. It is not surprising that themes such as coherence, happiness, self-betrayal and love recur constantly in María do Cebreiro's poems and that these connect intimately with processes such as learning, thought and study, which are of equal weight in her work.

This preoccupation with affects as/and cognition crystallizes in her book *Non queres que o poema te coñeza* [You don't want the poem to know you] (2004) and takes on a new direction in *I am not from here* (2008). The 2004 collection constantly alludes to the possibility of knowledge and comprehension through affect-guided stimuli and a will to explore the possibility of a 'flexible nonlinguistic account of cognition' (Nussbaum 2001:7). Granted, the body provides one possible pathway to

11

knowledge and understanding, but so too may one's wish to acknowledge the limitations of traditional forms of cognition and to recognise bewilderment as a state of liberation:

> 'At the beginning I had always to search for some detail among the papers.
> I thought that my disorderly approach was a problem,
> that I would never find what I was looking for
> amid piles and piles of sheets
> until I understood suddenly
> that it was my fingertips that were guiding me
> for they wanted to learn things independently.' (2004:37)[3]

The poet voluntarily places herself in a position of non-knowledge and tests her senses for consciousness. The loci where intellectual discernment will occur are not simply poetry, writing or stern deliberation, for as the poet will put it in *I am not from here*: 'poetry is not the space of the possible' (2008:19). Beyond such reflective processes, there is the value of prolonging the encounter with what is alien, seldom with an epiphanic point of closure in mind. The tempo and cadence of a foreign language, which is playfully 'courted' but never apprehended, the discovery that polysemy too is a culture-bound concept, or that calligraphy is a medium with which to dialogue with the world: these are some of the cognitive possibilities for traversing the edges between self and others and the affective spaces that connect and compound us. For similar reasons, traditional artifacts of knowledge transmission (books, letters, historical discourse) are endowed with an excess of meaning which crosses over to the realm of affectivity. Books do not simply convey but converse with knowledge, and they are also the richly textured objects of emotions. And so the poetic voice yearns for an affective connection that uses the intellectual space provided by the poem on the page as a starting line: 'This book you have in your hands today/ how I'd love to see it all underlined' (2004:125).

And so this book you have in your hands today continues to reflect on these lines of thought and others. Specifically, *I am not from here* reveals a preoccupation with affects and place, a need to move beyond an ontology and into a geography of affects. And again the body provides us with a point of departure, for the focus here is not on the corporeal manifestations of affects. The question is no longer the internal location of the effects of grief, love, fear or sexuality, imprinted on the body in the form of a trembling of the stomach, a convulsion, a shiver. There is, on the contrary, a preoccupation with how the body moves along, creating and shaping in its movement an affective map that has little to do with expected notions of bond and location. Granada, Seixas, Amsterdam, A Coruña, Bangor: and in between them a searching intellect wanders purposefully, envisioning a love in and of displacement.

In previous books (and in her work as both an academic and a literary translator), María do Cebreiro has considered the possibility of untranslatability. For a poet who does not shun notions such as truth and exactitude, this is not so surprising. I have, however, approached the task of translating *I Am Not from Here* with an unsettling sense of ease, perhaps because I was translating into my third language, with all the narrow margin for playfulness that this was allowing me. Like María, I still have family in a region of inland Galicia known as Terra Chá (Flat land), in the province of Lugo. I have touched the core of the bread, which is placed carefully under the wraps and left there to ferment. I have travelled far away from that core and savoured its necessary sourness. Its yeast-like qualities have also helped me grow. But in translating María do Cebreiro's poems I have not drawn on this affinity through a shared place and the emotional weight it evidently has for both of us. In other words, I am not from here either, but that is beside the point. María do Cebreiro's poetry has spoken to me in ways that have little to do with origins. It is the gift of her searching and sensitive intellect, her sincere regard for earnestness in her work and the work of others that have led me to heartening encounters with intellectual curiosity and rigour. Reading her poetry has always been part of those encounters; translating it has been a bonus. It is for this reason that I present the poems below not as a translation *of* but a translation *for* María do Cebreiro. As a gift, that is.

Notes

[1] In this realisation I draw inspiration from Galician poet Chus Pato, who, during a poetry recital at the Verbum museum (Vigo) in May 2009, said that her heavy heart was always made lighter when reading philosophy.
[2] For a brief explanation of this distinction see Sedgwick 2003:19–22.
[3] My translation from the original Galician.

Cited References:

Clough, Patricia Ticineto *The Affective Turn: Theorizing the Social*, Durham & London: Duke University Press, 2007.
Kosofsky Sedgwick, Eve *Touching Feeling: Affect, Pedagogy, Performativity*, Durham & London: Duke University Press, 2003.
Nussbaum, Martha C. *Love's Knowledge: Essays on Philosophy and Literature*, New York & Oxford: Oxford University Press, 1990.
Nussbaum, Martha C. *Upheavals of Thought: The Intelligence of Emotions*, Cambridge: Cambridge University Press, 2001.
Rábade Villar, María do Cebreiro *Non queres que o poema te coñeza*, Santiago de Compostela: Caixanova/Penclube, 2004.
—— 'Nuestro cuerpo es un campo de batalla: El sentido político de la poesía gallega escrita por mujeres', in M. Palacios and H. González (eds) *Palabras Extremas: Escritoras gallegas e irlandesas de hoy*, A Coruña: Netbiblo, 2008. pp.99–107.
—— *Non son de aquí*, Vigo: Xerais, 2008.
Weisman, Alan *The World Without Us*, New York: Thomas Dunne Books, 2007.

In memory of my grandfather Xosé

But poets should
Exert a double vision, should have eyes
To see near things as comprehensively
As if afar they took their point of sight,
And distant things as intimately deep
As if they touched them.

Elizabeth Barrett Browning, *Aurora Leigh*.

Bangor

Don't forget to bring your heart.
But I was left wondering about the wind's habits.

2

We lose what's ours,
not one step further
than this rain.

Further up north,
I close my hands.

He touched my fingers.

3

On his woollen jumper
the map of a language
with no army.

Neither pure, nor injured.

What's the point of hunger?

4
Ireland's potatoes
do not shoot.

What's the point of hunger?

5
To the north of what I'd never imagined
there's a man lying down.

He closes his hands.

I touch his fingers
one by one
and it doesn't add up.

6
Sheep in Wales
do not shoot.

Sometimes you see numbers on them.

7
He never folds into sleep.

You want me to be free
and you don't let me.

8
Stateless nations are windy.

Amarante

*The contraction between earth
and humidity we call wheat.*

1
Everything ends,
we said,
but bodies
explode
with waiting
and they bear
in secret
the long long course
of civilizations
river-like
summed up
between the wind's fingers
and this door
where you read
please
don't disturb
open
nevertheless
for you,
always

but sometimes
I shoot
I twist
inside
for I know
that a part
of me
will be destroyed
and no matter
how I try
I shall never know
which one.

2

In each contraction
there's an element
of hope
and catastrophe.
The small
events of passion
march back
to the mud:
there are no shapes:
there's life,
an attack
on what we currently
understand
by family.
Grain too
will be replaced.
The corn girl will come after
the steel girl,
the wood
after the Black Forest.
The reckless wind, perhaps

they'll want to give it
a place
name:
pretty maybe,
but still a treason.
And at the tip of your toes
there's the love for that girl
who managed to join your twenties
with my thirties,
and the ten years
in between
a big enough space
to be able to say
it was lovely and it lasted
what it had to last, till we hear
that there will always
be someone
to teach us
the meaning of time.
All relationships
are long distance but I am not
from here and I leave
no descendants,
I want no other origin
than this bridge
for as long as it holds us
and when it falls down
let us be noble and walk away
through the debris,
let us know how to part,
let it be as beautiful
as ever.

3

Do you know what shone
the most
in the distance?
It was in your hand
and it wasn't my scent,
it shone just as
the edge
of the sheets
of Rosalía de Castro's books
printed in Bible
paper. It shone
almost as much
as your words.
You'd like
not to be from here
but you're not going to swap
what's old for what's new.
You won't believe
that the poems
I write to you
can collide
with the wall
of the world.
Power is this:
a circle.
She has already understood
for us and for ever
that the words of love sprawl
and beg the rich
for a penny
at the Court's door. Property
is this:
what's yours is mine
and what's mine is everybody's:

what do I want
a house for
when I have no walls,
and who can carry you
and to what point
when the moment comes
our resistance
to saying no
will make us lose
each other.

4

It could well not be like this,
but poetry
is not
the space of the possible
and yet
Amarante
what a beautiful name
it could be a man or a woman,
the name of something
that never was.
Love is this:
the new.
It can just not happen
for centuries
then disappear
in seconds,
it can heal,
bleed through its wound,
breathe through its mouth,
rekindle the old flame
in the fire, make the volcano's womb
grow.

Will you ever come back to Santiago?

Take me wherever you go, like stars take
their music, and inside the hollow of your hands,
moist and warm, where I can stay and listen
to what you say in delight, eyes wide open,
knowing that our deeds often
cannot be dictated by our desires,
that parents, too, depend on their children,
armies, women on their side of the bed,
the things that we abandon only to cry at their loss
down the telephone line. Still some love though,
so much in fact that I cannot measure what I'm missing
or know whether I am outside or if it's rained.
But there's room for you still in the first seconds
of each thought and in the deepest land
of dreams that broke, and in the last memory,
inside a car eyes like headlights
facing a coastline that was never possible.
You my ship's captain: where is the signal?
If I bite you, will you respond? There's an endless war
and survivors lose their place, which was
the place of the other, where the body can only distinguish
the stitches in its clothes, but inside is naked
as it was before its birth. Take me home.

A Dutch nobleman (Golden Age)

In terrains we slowly stole from the sea,
terrains that give us
the growing measure of our loss,
a lack of agreement
which painters tried to reflect
there where the tissue folds,
in the embroidered flowers of the gorgets.
We are noble by blood
and facts will repeatedly
disprove us.
Who knows, perhaps
the sterility of our hearts
will arouse compassion in those who listen.
Who knows, when this reaches you
we may still be living off the rent, as we do now.
I'm not asking for sympathy,
I claim little for myself,
not even the knowledge
that we don't deserve a thing
should arouse your compassion.
There's a touch of aristocracy
in this wish of mine:
keep your resistance upright

like the edge of a sword,
indifferent to the loneliness of poppies
amid the wheat.

Rúa da Agriña

Staring is not free anymore,
the world is
full of sequences,
if they feed you
you feel hungry,
you are free
while you are asleep:
then you put on
your trousers,
you drag your chains.
But I can tell you
our flesh
is golden.
It will not rot.
Skulls are
so interesting.
It's true,
the desert
is inside our brother's
heart.
That's why work
shapes us inside.
Amid children's sheets

and books all around
the walls.
A party and no punishment.
Friendship is having
a place to sleep.
Vivienne Eliot
danced
in foxtrot
clubs, Jean
Verdenal
bred dead-earth lilies
and neither she
nor he made him
happy.
'There's no God
but there's
the soul'.
And I too know
that praying
is a different thing.
My father on his part
read Marx
('Language is consciousness').
At school, during the break
his daughter
would speak
Castilian.
'Are you trying to be
one of the alienated?'
I still
wonder today
whether his prophecy
was fulfilled.

Castelao Avenue, no number.

You gave me a home
and more importantly:
the sense of loss,
the certainty
that whatever we possess
can be threatened
living as we do
with the exact knowledge
that we will always be
about to leave.

(Poems go with you
and touch you
differently
each time).

A Coruña

It was so windy
that I lost
my memory.
The earth is
divided
in two.
We inhabit
the side
of desolation.
But we can say:
we love
the desert.
I am your
labyrinth.
Rejoice, rejoice,
you are the only
thing
in the world
that comes back.

The country of memory

Republic of the souls
who left
with their head held high,
at the foot of our hands.
Life also knows
of borders.
But the dead don't live
just because we remember them,
they don't live in the smoke
or inside the urns
or in the rotten wood
or in the whitewashed walls
or in love.
They live in themselves
and they judge us
and they don't dictate
our thought,
but our acts.

San Roque hospital

It's true, we both left
January so far behind
that we can't possibly
forget it.
The day it ends
we'll sit on the bench
that best knows me
and you will say again:
I don't need my eyes
to see you.
And I will say that portraits
have a frame.
And deeper inside?
The two of us.
I was already by your side,
don't you ever
send me the photos
of the places we trod upon together
unknowingly.
There's clay in my hair.
Each month. It's quite stubborn,
it goes away slowly.
We're lucky today,

waxing crescent,
time to sow the red earth
of your arms.
We will not found anything.
We will honour the limits.
We will love the ground for what it is.

Doyenne of death

She knows how to kill,
I stare at the cuts.
I know how to spread the sheets.
I know how to close the eyes
of the dead.
But now the shutters
of what I once sought
are down, a part of me
remains there,
a part that hurts.
Whoever knows the tasks of old age
moves more lightly.
I still walk slowly.
When the doyenne of death
gives me her hand,
I look elsewhere,
I join day and night together
in my fingers,
I kiss the door
and the window panes.

The quiet man

Where are we, really
when we listen to music?
You were there standing still, still tense,
your back interrupted
on the asphalt.
Like Maureen O'Hara
forever still
before the infinite
task of language,
in the first words.
Salvador de Mosteiro,
the land of cherries.
She still remembers
how she didn't want to go to school,
she still remembers her fear
of not being understood.
We are doomed to be free.
We never learn.
After so much resistance to this job,
what is the true
age of language?
We don't want to leave
that vertebra.

If it breaks, as little as it is,
everything breaks.
It's our resistance
to changing states,
to capital. 'I don't want
to know this city',
you said, and so
we invented neighbourhoods.
The guerrilla was not
a public space.
It took me a while to grasp
that my father avoided
open spaces
and dark rooms.
It took me a while to grasp why
my cousin María
dos Anxos
cried in that flat in A Coruña:
'There it comes, the tractor of Casa Nova!'.
It took me a while to grasp
the sharp fear of cities.
'Guilt is defeat,
just like despair'. The quiet man
burnt down. He wasn't Homeric.
Emotions are not what's personal.
Falling asleep, getting up,
a tumour under your arm,
the age of memories.
That's why my duty was to go out and buy
a travel guide of a place I've never been,
and where I have no intention
of going.
Those who so stubbornly search for the truth
deserve the punishment of finding it.

Still waters

To let things remain
behind
like fine flour
sticking to our fingers
or see them run
like river sand through a sieve.
And life in between.
Draining.
To say human
kind: clumsiness,
pretence.
These were images I conjured
just to come nearer
to the possibility of losing,
the real impossibility
of wordplay.
Desire, despair.
After all, there's nothing
we can't avoid
and yet
we finally abandon
so many things
once made to last
from cowardice or slovenliness.

Madrid

And also my cousin Elvira's
spine.
Curved like a question mark.
A condition she inherited.
Fear.
Doctors'
dogged will to bend us.
Exercise sequences.
Things she couldn't
eat.
We visited her.
(Madrid).
A first impression:
an intermittent
Schweppes sign.
'No element in this book
can be detached
from its dedication.'
At night, back at the lodging
a dripping tap.
Water was a treasure.
I didn't sleep.
Then in the morning,

a sachet of decaf,
froth, hot milk
that mum made me
drink spoon by spoon.
Blow on it to cool it down,
drink it slowly,
pour the liquid
into another mug.
Those were the habits,
our family heritage:
always let boiling milk turn
lukewarm.

Crime and splendour

Treated as we have been
since childhood
in that laconic style
of those who are fond of us
but not to the bone,
nobody taught us how to receive.
And that thing bright as sunlight
before which even the flames
would stop flickering,
that thing said to be better
than any other,
that thing was ignored, for we resolved
that nothing so splendid
could have been made for us.

Lisboa, 2006

We said of foreign lands
that they weren't a country.
Far from everywhere,
how can we measure the age
of nations?
There's no point expecting
them to listen.
Inside or outside,
who can do anything at all?
We are not certain.
We are thirsty.

In the meantime, trains go by.
Goods.
Sometimes, even cattle.
It's hot and we're blessed
by the beggars in the underground.
'Good save you, sweetheart'.
Barely a formula.
Who wants salvation
when there can be loss?
'So much people had died
there in Spain'. Galicia

is not Spain. She doesn't speak
of colonies. She has no energy left.

The devout women got off
at the first station,
for Sunday mass,
so many years ago.
We're at the end of our tether.
They abolished pity
(that wasn't a bad thing, in fact).
But not even.

On the art critic's
yellow shirt
I played word puzzles.
It wasn't an anagram.
It's all too clear: YSL.
Did anyone say *no logo*?
He's a teacher, comes from far away.
And what do I care?
He'll only watch
Oliveira's films.

Confusing things feel familiar.
An invitation or a threat?
Bottomless roots.
Do not fool yourselves:
There are no sister languages,
and you need some style
to make a taxi
stop at your feet.
But public transport
won't stop for all the world's gold.

Working classes,
we devour leftovers.
There's no weekend.
There's no end.

Autumn poem

There was always the temptation
to give in. (The heated
war. The rush.)
You were in Russia
looking intently at everything.
It hadn't dawned yet.
In the landscape, excuses
to warm up,
to continue.
Then winter came.
February is fickle
and you never know.
I looked inside myself:
I've come such a long way.

Ponte da Lima

My grandfather came to the south.
We shared
a seat.
When we were small, love
meant travelling in discomfort.
'You study
just like your father used to.'
Studying is not reading.
But the sheets would shine
inside our green car.
What my grandfather saw
was not the book.
It was the absorption.
The indifference.
He then gave me
his arm. Nothing bad
could happen to me.

('And what will you ask of me
that I can't give you?'
said the little girl to the monster.
And the monster replied:
'That you learn to speak
my language'.)

Granada

There's no home, if it rains.
That was the condition
for holidaying.
Two families,
one apartment,
a one-off rent
payment
and already on the afternoon serial
a mention
of her illness.
Godmother, so young,
could not process
food.
She was a perfectionist.
Did she think it
unworthy of her mouth?
Again and again she sized herself up
and placed the tape measure
on its side.
The path of crime
intersects with the hero's,
the traitor's with epic.
And remember: 'The Pays

Basque n'est pas à vendre'.
The Moor
handed over his keys
and cried.
They say a continent
cannot be discovered.
But then, is it impossible
to lose a city?
Oh my dear Alama.
Elvira.
Is the destruction
of others
what makes us strong
or do we become strong
in spite
of their destruction?

Lugo

And that was Becerreá: well-worn
brick. A closed-off
road
that they'd always call
general. Migrants
returned from the Basque Country.
They claimed to understand
terrorism.
Thanks to some film at the pub
I learnt the word *picoleto*.
And on the subsequent days,
how green was my valley,
heaven will judge her,
and so on.
The house in the barracks,
a salute to the sun,
Afonso,
my first
embrace (not in order,
but in love).
Those cousins of ours
who lived in A Coruña
and would use the words

they found in magazines.
'Every morning in the world
is a one-way journey.'
It's as if places
could preserve
their memory.
As if they remembered
the things that people
don't want to remember.
'Iran, my golden country',
'Night-time consolation'.
Those were the words of the woman exile,
as little as she was, and now
I add:
Seixas or Becerreá,
glass with no bevelled edge,
deep and
yellow, a locked
dining-room and the furniture
almost always
covered with drapes.
The Day of the Dead.
The visits.
We heal the past
just like that, as it comes,
no soap and with our backs to it.
From behind.

Speed dating

The old argument
about humanism
and war on capital.
The glass fell to the floor.
It was so soft
that she didn't want
to resort to dialectics.
Globalisation,
disconcertedness.
We'll be left in doubt.
They'd left fruit stones
in the shop window
so that they could flourish.
Since it's all in the open
no one says a word.
But do tell me,
what will we do tomorrow,
when we wake up
at the root
of the verb *to flourish*?

Sintra

Every small place has a name.
They live well. They sell things.
Mother-of-pearl, glass,
manufactured goods
antique shops
in case we get bored of the present.
But let's keep moving.
Can a new world be created
from such a concentrated
act of looking?
Silver legends
drip down the walls.
Rain doesn't know of corruption.
It always loves open rifts.
Ferns leave a trail,
and let the day tell
its story.
There are museums full of toys,
doll hospitals.
Children devise strategies
on the game board.
So much tin sheets and what for?
This was war, an assault.

My friend said:
'Chestnut shells are still green'.
The truth is that things
are spiky
and parks are places
for the weekend.
My love being on the other side of the line,
how am I supposed to like
poplar parks?
Well you'll have to close them down.
But when? I asked.
What do I know, you replied.
Tourism, terrorism.

On the things we keep inside

From the outside, it describes,
and discloses things.
From the outside
it stops at the inner core.
One has to go
far away in order to see.
When we arrive
we see:
there's no bottom.
She goes alone but she loves us.
She opens the door pane
and whispers:
gaskets don't really need us,
all walls
wear out
and wood
ends up giving way.
But fallen beams
can burn too.

Biscaia (the Law of the Father)

And even when amorous choices can be made without any
external conditioning, the result tends to depend all the same
on personal intrusions that are no less obscure: vanity, fear,
rivalry, an error of judgement.

She always imagines
that her father
injects venom
and stones travel
down the veins,
the memory of the species,
habits and signals,
wine that tastes like unfermented
grapes.
A dry river. Threadless
needles, and no thimble.
Since I was little, I have searched for
my garden:
a fence they painted
yellow,
wild rosebushes,
the thornless kind.
My idea of homeland.
dark cigarettes from that mouth

that made me learn
it all by force.
When I couldn't swallow
the smoke. Is homeland
a state of plenitude, communism?
A homeland is, like love,
the daughter of absolute misery
and extravagance.
It smells musty,
we love what's hurtful,
and never wake up alone:
A room for three.
Why don't we write down
everything we learn about
sweet surrender,
about the centres of pain
and pleasure?
Flesh is not weak,
flesh is tender,
and the river that carries us
is death.
There is no double trust,
I don't know whether
I'll write poetry again,
it's not true that a name
can help restore identity,
it's not true that a language
can limit us through silence.
We sleep on our backs.
You have to be brave
to wake up naked.
People don't chose
who to love,
they love whoever they find
along the way.

Homeland, your eyes are
neither hazel nor honey.
And you have no pupil,
only iris.
You are not a woman who cries
as she washes her sex
with her tears, and dries it
with the thread of her hair.
I was always ready to flee,
even when
I was with people I was already fleeing.
But we will keep loving each other
with no emergency plan,
and no sofa. *Take my hand,*
take my hand,
this land is made for you.

Down the hill

On those hospital days,
broken
nights,
rivers,
leafless elder trees,
milk parties,
insects so blue,
how is a forest
created?
My hands are
quick.
They don't give.
I hate you,
soft mountains.
The moon is always
waning.
The opposite of love
is disdain.
Hatred,
with different
hands.
But both of them
build things

down the hill
and remain
formally
excluded
from here.
And be it
known that I sign
this contract
on your lips
but we'll tear it up
afterwards:
This is a homeless
love,
you cannot
keep it.
The wind is
wild, it says something
we can't see
and all the papers blow away,
all at once
it makes us learn
that we
need no
witnesses.

North

The rain was the judgement
and we were the penalty.
I paid for my part
without a second thought.
As for the city, it gave us
exactly the same.
We've come here so often.
I wouldn't get lost
even if blind-folded,
but I'd rather keep my eyes open
to see you.
I count the hours.
I'm in your coach,
you're in my train.
It rains and rains
but we never get wet.

A grove (Compostela)

Along the Crescent's grove
I saw a shepherdess walk,
at a distance from the crowd
louder and louder she sang,
seizing the folds of her dress
as the sun rays
sat, on the banks of the river Sar.
Johan Airas.

'I want you to be free'.
And what if I'm not?
Freedom in anger,
freedom. Things happen
up in the mountain,
cars pull aside.
Loners look
at couples.
'Fever is a place.'
Inside one's heart
there are no words.
We love epilepsy
under the chestnut trees,
and in the sun's arms.
Even if none of this

is true
come here and I'll tell you
what being apart means
in full,
the roughness of the skin,
the soap bar thinning down
on its dish
and how the clothes
that were not complaining before
now drip dry on their line.
But behind the stitches,
loose threads join
the bleeding parts together.
One can go on,
look ahead.
Something died inside you.
You can go through life
if you caress
the bird that dwells
in the back of your neck.
There was no land before.
They buried the birds
after the body.
The origins of memory.
Restless blood.
Exclamation signs
underneath your eye-lashes.
Music: the generations'
shared soul.
Roots grow where you are,
where you are, for I don't have them.
Will you ever come back
to Santiago?

Winter scene (Amsterdam)

And just as the problem with painting
is light, the problem with life
is shadows.
What can we do with shadows?
What can we do
against the invasive power
of surveillance?
The internalization
of habits and costumes.
Official couples.
A more difficult thing:
that a dromedary threads
the fat in its bump
through a needle.
Caryatids cover their faces
with their hands.
At that point I understand
the meaning of affliction.
As distant from pain
as pleasure
is from litter and
the weeping women of Cangas
from Aphrodite.

The weight of reality
cannot be questioned,
yet in the meantime
we,
while we're at it,
shall create
a terrorist group
for the liberation
of love.

Valdavara Cave (Cruzul)

Before coming out in the light,
after entering the caves.
The fair-haired man
would give us one hundred pesetas
if we learnt the names
of the Goth kings by heart.
Was it a fair deal?
In Cruzul, the fugitive
who hid around the caves
was also the fugitive
who had to learn to reappear.
A love story
told so many times
that we forget
it all happened in the year '38
when a man
on his way to the front
did not notice her crossing.
That seamstress,
the prettiest woman
in the Ancares region,
was left crippled and came back,
married my grandfather

and so now I write.
Herodotus tells
of how Xerxes
meant to beat up the sea.
3000 masts.
Blood-thirsty wind
in his eyes.
But the sea has no coast.
Therein lies the cause
of our frustration.
History, history you
are not the master of anything.
In an interview, the subject
is the one asking the questions.
Now they say
that a scrawny little boy
was our ancestor.
Please give their health back
to those who are alive,
and their dead to those who remember
and leave the crowns
for the saints
('Blessed be the home
where the image
of my heart
is displayed and honoured.')
Time makes the engraved letters disappear.
'I can't separate
your soul from mine,'
he said. That has not disappeared.
And you are the most powerful animal
in the Earth's entrails.

García Rodríguez

The chemist's head.
The tower.
The thermal power station.
He wanted to give himself away
to the children of his children.
They didn't have any.
A fear of containers.
A pyramidal use
of violence.
The chemist's head.
The company's store.
The tower.
His skin
was so pale
that an aspirin
destroyed him.
Blood did not
clot.
Sperm that didn't set
rose up eventually,
in the form
of a haemorrhage.
Endesa, Reganosa,

your stations
always needed
his intelligence.
Yet all the wretched
men
deserve better.

The bread's core

I threw the bread's core,
The part always kept under wraps,
inside the basket
while the basket carries
a whole life,
a book,
the phrase I heard:

'The world will end
when everything is covered with paths.'

I threw the bread's core moulded by the fingers,
the part to be shared by the family,
the part that helped those who were born to grow,
the part that will help to be born those who haven't
been yet.

I never demanded
the peasants' triumph of you,
to be able to manage the grain
under the autumn sun.
Do you know of a greater arrogance
than to grow under the sun?

Although linen sticks to it,
I want the bread's core,
the part divided
by the fingers,
the part that will be shared
among the people,
the part that will help
what hasn't happened yet to grow,
the winter's wool, the bread's core
left to ferment, at home.

All the world's gold

It felt as if the body knew a secret. As if there was something hidden
amid the bones, blood and flesh, the secret of time or life, something
that cannot be said to others or translated into any other language,
because words would not stand it.

Who said that being a coward was easy?
Those of us whose courage has failed
know that the job
requires perseverance,
that's why cowardice awaits at our doorstep
with a wax board
for us to etch our debts on
until we stumble somehow on truth.
Those of us who have once touched its face
know that cowardice will always understand us
and with a free hand, after taking our money,
it will tell us we're right. May the poem
protect us from vengeance.
May it save us, if it can, from allegorical reason
and with a busy hand let it sow for us
ounces and ounces of patience.
In nameless spaces, with numbers on the door,
homeless rooms, physical places,
sometimes the moment arises

when we sit in front of each other
and realise our mutual impossibility.
Because whatever passes through a body, right until the end,
bears the significance of a restitution,
just as electricity can keep its place
and not just that shiver of the feet
when it touches us. Humility please save us,
you whose name sounds like earth. Don't reach
for glory, don't expect to stay there.
This is what I said and it became the truth.
But not because words can rise above
what they always are, truncated air and matter,
but because whoever understands first
leaves first.
From all this we derive a total contempt
for goods,
not for what we earn,
but for its easy show,
accumulations, so opposed
to the composure with which the powerful vent their anger
knowing that strength feeds itself on rules and not on capital,
unaware of the wire
that brings lovers together then separates them,
bound to the refuse generated by those movements
destined to make things be understood
without words.
From this we derive a contempt for the vulgar woman,
who hides her treasure
in the folds of her skirt
just to perpetuate the cleaner's
fractional salary ad infinitum,
and that bastard logic in the question:
'Can I possibly help you with that?'
The reply was no,
for the things worth our while

are always doomed to sudden death
like glasses crashing in our hands.
But experience told me:
Try not to write
a moral poem. And so I've tried.
All the world's gold
isn't worth your skin next to mine.
Tears won't make the trees grow
and the girl who wants to be a river
will not be able to escape from the thread of music
that tightens the seven muscles of sadness.
That is the exact nature of what the mill in our heart
(which washes the grain and doesn't hit back)
has chosen.

And she did not choose the homeland

1

One day, a woman
wrote a poem about a fish.

Her clothes were the net.
A monument to water.
Remember?

It wasn't at all like being born again.
It was as if she and I were alive without having been born.

2

And then he came along.
And she was left loving gaps forever.

3

He said: there's no homeland
if you're far away.
And she did not choose the homeland.

He said: there's no sleep
if you never doze off.
And she did not want the bed.

He said there's no thirst
if you touch me.
And she didn't want her hands.

4
Life, she thought
will do as she pleases with you and me.
Each of us in our bed,
common places.
'I don't want to hurt you.'
The things they said
did not preclude anything.
They went to bed, hurt each other,
went back to square one.

5.
And for each experience,
there's a mark on the skin.
An invisible one, though.
Look at me, can't you see it?
You can close your eyes,
and it doesn't go away.
I could just not see you again,
carry you inside.